THE WORLDS OF ARCHITECTURAL DIGEST

CALIFORNIA INTERIORS

THE WORLDS OF ARCHITECTURAL DIGEST

CALIFORNIA INTERIORS

EDITED BY PAIGE RENSE

EDITOR-IN-CHIEF, ARCHITECTURAL DIGEST

THE KNAPP PRESS   PUBLISHERS   LOS ANGELES

THE VIKING PRESS   DISTRIBUTORS   NEW YORK

Published in the United States of America in 1979
The Knapp Press
5900 Wilshire Boulevard, Los Angeles, California 90036
Copyright © 1979 by Knapp Communications Corporation
All rights reserved

Distributed by The Viking Press
625 Madison Avenue, New York, New York 10022

Distributed simultaneously in Canada by Penguin Books Canada Limited

Library of Congress Cataloging in Publication Data
Main entry under title: California interiors.
(The Worlds of Architectural digest)
Selections from the pages of Architectural digest, newly edited and designed.
1. Interior decoration — California. I. Rense, Paige.
II. Architectural digest. III. Series.
NK2002.C34   1979   747'.8'83   79-84685

ISBN 0-89535-045-9
Printed and bound in the United States of America

CONTENTS

FOREWORD

Today in the United States there is an intriguing myth that every new fashion and trend and way of life begins in California, eventually spreading to other parts of the country. Surely this is a heady draft for Californians and conjures up once more images of a new world and the adventurous frontier.

If these are comforting thoughts to Californians, however, they do not seem to me to apply in any large sense to the field of interior design. Do not misunderstand. This is by no means a negative statement. It is simply that there are so many different Californias represented in the following pages it would be impossible to say with accuracy that any given trend in interior design began — or begins — in California.

In any case, trends have never been the concern of ARCHITECTURAL DIGEST, and this will be more than apparent as you look at the various houses and apartments in the present volume, all selected and adapted from past issues of the magazine. The task I have always given my editors and writers and photographers has been simply to report, to reveal the many different faces of life in every part of the country and the world. In limiting this particular volume to California interiors, there is really no other purpose than to present a cornucopia of styles — styles ranging from the most traditional to the most contemporary, influences ranging from the Spanish to the Victorian.

The state is a large one, generous and filled with extreme contrasts of nature. There is the desert and the mountain, the lake and the ocean; there are torrential rains and almost eternal sunlight; there are contrasts without end. And the ways people live in California and the ways they have decorated their homes are as large and generous and as filled with contrast. Whatever the formality or informality of any individual design in the pages that follow, the emphasis is most certainly on comfort and the expression of personal freedom.

To be honest, of course, this quest for comfort and freedom is far from being uniquely Californian. It is, I think, apparent in every successful design, no matter how large or how small, no matter whether it is found in the United States or in Europe or in the Far East. What is unique about California is its abundant variety, and that variety may be considered a microcosm of the many styles and trends found in this country as a whole and in other parts of the world. It is a tiresome cliché to say that California was created yesterday. It has a past, and a rich one. But it seems to me true enough that California today reflects American life at almost its best and most inclusive. It is a land where the majesty of nature and the art of man-made décor have been harmoniously and casually combined, where design is appropriate to the land. It is essentially American — and essentially Californian.

Paige Rense
Editor-in-Chief
Los Angeles, California

THE WORLDS OF ARCHITECTURAL DIGEST

CALIFORNIA INTERIORS

DRAMA OF THE UNEXPECTED

The mise-en-scène is Baroque but strangely simple. Ludwig of Bavaria would have been at home; so would Mondrian. On a table near the entrance of a designer's showroom in Los Angeles is a French magazine open to the photograph of a study in Paris: a glass writing surface supported by stainless steel, behind it a flamboyant Empire chair in scarlet, and behind them both a wall decorated with Oriental magnificence. Interior designer Sally Sirkin Lewis, who owns the showroom with her husband, is very fond of the photograph. It is not her work, although it is her style: unexpected and disciplined.

She sits in a simple white chair, surrounded by the appointments she loves. The background is rich, alive with arabesques and convoluted forms. There are Moorish columns, palm fronds, animal horns set in plastic, Chinese dragons, primitive African sculpture and stylized paintings from India. Brown suede is much in evidence, as is the color white — white lampshades and bases and mirror frames and soft couches accented with bright pillows of startling Javanese design. It is an Eastern bazaar, and many a caravan must have crossed the desert sands to bring these riches to Melrose Avenue. The effects are surprising, theatrical, hovering on the edge of decadence — but elegant, controlled. Always controlled, for this designer believes in basic simplicity, punctuated by the exotic and the unusual. With a certain stubbornness, she will not deal with clients who are unable to share her own sophistication and awareness. In a harmonious relationship with the right person, she would rather plan one small room than twenty thousand square feet of space. She finds it essential to establish a firm basis of understanding between herself and her clients. But such understanding, she admits, is "a two-way street," and everyone concerned must have an open mind.

Originally from New York, she first came to Los Angeles to design a showroom, with no thoughts of staying. At the time, her career focused on corporate designing, and she had served her apprenticeship in a number of architectural offices. In the company of architects she learned many basic skills that she still uses: an understanding of lighting, for example, and the ability to read blueprints. Today, it is her habit to make a blueprint for every new interior, no matter how small. In this way she is able to capture what seem to her the key elements in design: "totality and a feeling for the whole."

Her preference for the strong statement and her belief in the importance of the relationship between client and designer are apparent in the house she designed for the Harris L. Katlemans of Beverly Hills. It is dramatic and full of surprises, yet basically simple, comfortable and functional. If some of the results are theatrical, they were surely intended to be. The designer recalls a few points of disagreement with Mrs. Katleman, but minor differences were soon settled. "Trust me," said Sally Sirkin Lewis. "Everything will be right." And it is.

"There really are no rules," the designer says, and her work on the Katleman residence is an affirmation of that point of view. It is also — with its unusual fabrics and exotic paintings and striking mirrors — the affirmation of what may well be the designer's credo: "I like strength, the strong statement, not weak or simply pretty things."

For this reason, though she greatly emphasized the use of contemporary furniture in this Beverly Hills house, she was careful to make it eclectic in the best, and most personal, sense. The house now has something of the mystery and glamour of her own showroom, a vigorous mixture of the contemporary, the exotic and the unexpected.

PRECEDING PAGE: *Illustrating the happy coexistence of simplicity and opulence in the Beverly Hills home Sally Sirkin Lewis designed for the Harris L. Katlemans, Jim Silvester's contemporary painting* Dust *backs an intricately carved Baroque gilded console with a marble top.*

BELOW: *An Indian painting, Chinese porcelains and mounted ostrich eggs counterpoint the Living Room's sleek pillowed banquettes.* BOTTOM: *Paneling, a bay window and a marble fireplace add traditional architectural detail to the predominantly contemporary Den.*

LEFT: *Tonal contrasts enliven the dark hues of the Living Room: A James Maxwell abstract painting punctuates one wall, and orchids add another bright note.* BELOW LEFT: *The Sitting Room features a lively range of textures, including a lacquered ceiling, straw-covered walls, suede-upholstered sofa and ottoman, and satin-covered pillows. Even the patterned carpet suggests a variegated surface.* BELOW: *A chandelier, delicate as a spray of flowers, glows above rounded chairs set rhythmically around the glass-topped Dining Room table.*

OPPOSITE: *A rustic twisted-branch four-poster bed points up the varied accents of flowered chintz, plaid taffeta, a gleaming jade disc and a gilded grotto chair in the Master Bedroom. Stacked cushions repeat and reverse the step motif of geometric bedside consoles.* ABOVE: *Wicker furniture, batik-upholstered pillows, Chinese garden seats and a profusion of plants make the Patio a verdant oasis.*

THE PAST IS PRESENT

Spero Arbes, who lives in a San Francisco Victorian house, is not all that fond of things Victorian. But he took the best of what he found, and by adding and altering created a look that suits him very well. "When I bought the place," says the antiques dealer, "it looked like a haunted house. It was in a very run-down and neglected condition. But fortunately, nothing disastrous had been done to it, so I didn't have to undo someone else's revisions."

Built about 1887, the residence was originally a pair of flats, which in itself is unusual in an era of single-family construction. Mr. Arbes bought the structure in 1962, and at first all three floors housed his antiques shop. But a few years later he moved his business to Jackson Square and so decided to renovate the downstairs area and remodel it into a separate apartment. After sealing the connecting stairways and completing this first project, he began work on the top floor, where he had previously used three rooms for his living quarters.

Almost all the antique furniture in the house has been re-covered because, as Mr. Arbes explains, "you very seldom find anything still upholstered in the original fabric, and if you do, it's usually in shreds. The sofa in the front room still has the original tapestry on it, but it's so worn that I'm very careful of it. I have a cat that just loves to sleep on it, but I try to make sure that she stays out of the room."

In the living room the original Victorian fireplace has been replaced with a Georgian one, and flanked with bookcases. "The wainscoting was ugly; it was all that tongue-in-groove work. So I put tempered Masonite over it to smooth it out. Then I put on panels and added wall moldings. However, I did make sure to keep the original ceiling moldings."

The dining room is probably the warmest room in the house, with its soft terra-cotta walls reflecting the glow of the candles in the handsome old cathedral chandelier that dates back to the time of Louis XIII. "It is not wired, and I've kept the candles," explains the owner. "It gives an enormous amount of light when it's completely lit—almost too much for the size of the room. The chandelier is somewhat overscaled, but so is the buffet. I think using large things in a small room creates a great deal of interest and also deemphasizes the smallness of the space." The deck and the garden beyond are lighted at night, adding another dimension to the dinner parties that Mr. Arbes likes to give several times a month.

The décor in the house is of no definite period. "I've mixed it; it's just whatever I like. And I think it has turned out rather well. There are some Chinese artifacts, some Ming jars. The bust in the front room is a Roman antiquity. It's Commodus, the son of Marcus Aurelius, done when he was about fifteen. One tapestry I have goes back to the middle of the sixteenth century. Perhaps the 'newest' antique in the house is the Louis XVI bed, made about 1780. The only really modern piece is the sofa in the living room." Just as there is no adherence to any one style of furniture, so is the selection of woods diverse, with walnut, oak and mahogany, English, French and Italian furniture all mixed together.

"Naturally the rooms are all quite small, because they are typical Victorian rooms," says Mr. Arbes. "But that really doesn't bother me a great deal. The only problem is that I can't acquire more furniture, and I'm always finding pieces that I would like to keep. But with this house, when I add a piece of furniture, it means something else has to go. Then *that* means finding other pieces to go with it. It gets to be a merry-go-round. So in the last year and a half I've stopped acquiring things. I feel that I've finally put things together the way I want them."

European warmth pervades the Victorian home of San Francisco antiques dealer Spero Arbes. PRECEDING PAGE: *In the Living Room, a 17th-century tapestry adds visual grandeur.*

ABOVE: *In the Hallway, a 16th-century Dutch portrait of a lady overlooks a Charles II five-legged table. A cluster of Ming and Ch'ien Lung porcelains gives an Oriental air to the antique tableau.*

ABOVE: *A suede-covered chair near a glowing Georgian fireplace is an inviting spot for a restful hour of reading. Twin bookcases, holding a collection of early pewter pieces to counterbalance their orderly rows of books, flank a dignified late-17th-century portrait of Charles II.*
OPPOSITE: *Floor-to-ceiling French doors lend an illusion of space to the typically small Victorian Dining Room. The velvet-upholstered Louis XIII chairs that accompany the walnut refectory table repeat the warm tones of the Roman linen shades, dyed to closely match the walls.*

Pairs of giltwood Adam appliqués, velvet-covered pillows and antique silver candlesticks emphasize the graceful symmetry of a Library seating area. A Sir Peter Lely portrait presides with dignity.

In one corner of the library, a 16th-century Aubusson tapestry serves as a background for a Queen Anne walnut secretary. A marble bust of the emperor Commodus and a Louis XIII lectern accentuate the quiet and studious mood of the ensemble.

Another view of the Library reveals a George III pine overmantel mirror that visually extends the room. The vivid hues of an 18th-century Tekke Turkoman rug brighten the area, which is otherwise dominated by the deep, rich color of the velvet wallcovering.

An intricate millefleur tapestry framed in contemporary steel dramatizes the century-bridging mood of the Master Bedroom. A Roman bust, circa A.D. 300, rests on a massive Louis XIII walnut table. A view into the hall reveals a Sir Henry Raeburn portrait over a Jacobean chest.

REMODELING IS THE SOLUTION

This contemporary house, which was totally transformed by interior designer Stephen Chase, might well provide an interesting blueprint for the future. It is a unique demonstration of how to acquire a brand-new home — without moving an inch.

Like many another American couple with grown children, Mr. and Mrs. Arthur Shapiro of Beverly Hills wanted to sell the large house originally designed for them by architect Harold W. Levitt and move to smaller quarters. Even though the residence had been conceived as an elegant setting for a couple, it no longer conformed to the owners' needs; there were, for example, unused children's bedrooms. Mrs. Shapiro wanted to move into an apartment. Her husband, on the other hand, was reluctant since the restrictions of high-rise living did not appeal to him. A solution was necessary, and Stephen Chase provided it in the easiest way possible. He welcomed the challenge of transforming the house so completely that the owners would be happy to stay where they were. Like them, he admired its structural beauty, and he knew that anything comparable, whether condominium, apartment or new house, would be difficult to find. In addition, the location near Sunset Boulevard would be virtually impossible to match. The house was secluded, yet close to Mr. Shapiro's office and centrally situated for his wife's many activities. They both went along enthusiastically with Mr. Chase's concept of transformation.

The result is a house of quiet excitement, and the harmony and composition of each room become more apparent with each visit. Color, more than any other single factor, is responsible. "The house itself is so beautiful that we could have come in with any color scheme," says the designer, "such as blue, green, brown or the various earth tones we planned to use and did use to a certain extent. But the real excitement in the palette comes from the use of eggplant and lavender and purple — a striking blend of colors that the owners specified and that many Italian couture houses have used to great effect."

Indeed, an Italian influence is apparent throughout the house, and Mr. Chase drew inspiration from contemporary Italian designers in his search for appropriate furniture and accessories. He also introduced African art into several of the rooms. In fact, the owners' passion for art is reflected in a gallery gained by remodeling a large and formal dining room. The family room was turned into a convenient dining area furnished with two tables for four; each table can be readily expanded to seat as many as ten.

Mr. Chase is a diplomat and much too wise to call any design he has done his favorite, but his affection for this one is obvious. "I was able to buy things for the house that I would love to have myself. Take, for example, the giant African lizard sculpture on the living room wall next to the fireplace, or the buffalo skull on the other wall." His interest in the house was intense, and he went to great lengths to perfect each detail. With his own hands he crafted a finger painting for a lacquered chest in the master bedroom. Since he feels that extravagance is out of place today, his overall concern was to make the house seem smaller and less elaborate than it really is.

When the time came to present the owners with their new home, he took pains to dramatize the occasion. "I sent them to Palm Beach. Then I moved in and worked with a team for three days. I was quite nervous, since the family didn't know exactly what I had planned. True, they had given me carte blanche, but I had done unusual things. But when they walked in, I didn't have to ask a thing. The smiles on their faces told me all I wanted to know."

PRECEDING PAGE: *Great expanses of window reveal the cheerful contemporary interior of a Beverly Hills home designer Stephen Chase totally remodeled for Mr. and Mrs. Arthur Shapiro. The spacious, simplified structure was designed by architect Harold Levitt, the surrounding Japanese-inspired garden by landscape architect Jocelyn Domela.*

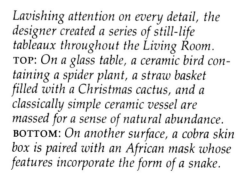

Lavishing attention on every detail, the designer created a series of still-life tableaux throughout the Living Room. TOP: *On a glass table, a ceramic bird containing a spider plant, a straw basket filled with a Christmas cactus, and a classically simple ceramic vessel are massed for a sense of natural abundance.* BOTTOM: *On another surface, a cobra skin box is paired with an African mask whose features incorporate the form of a snake.*

A carefully controlled palette unifies the comfortable living room. TOP: *Commodious Italian leather chairs are separated by a marble table.* BOTTOM: *The gleam of a bronze, glass and chrome table is underscored by a large geometric-patterned rug; in the background, an African lizard sculpture is suspended on a dark wall.* OPPOSITE: *Italian lamps of organic form illuminate a suede-upholstered wall highlighted by Roméo Reyna's bold tapestry.*

RIGHT: *The Entrance Hall offers a long vista through the residence. To the right is the gallery, which can be closed off by shoji screens.* FAR RIGHT: *The Gallery, which prior to remodeling served as a formal dining room, is now a plant-filled refuge for viewing works of art. A suede and Lucite bench offers a vantage point for contemplating Alan Davies's colorful painting.*

OPPOSITE: *Remodeling transformed the former family room into a flexible new Dining Area, where two expandable burl tables, surrounded by upholstered chrome-based chairs, can accommodate as many as 20 people; when occasion warrants, additional tables and chairs can be brought indoors from the terrace. Floral centerpieces on each table (seen in detail at left) enhance the color scheme that warms this room as well as the residence's other major living areas. Delicate blinds in the background screen the outdoor scene, endowing it with a diffused softness.*

A peaceful garden view adds serenity to the Master Bedroom, where sliding doors open onto one of several terraces. Inside, an Italian leather and chrome chair, with ottoman, is a perfect spot for relaxing; a television is discreetly concealed within the nearby cabinet.

RIGHT: *Lizard-patterned vinyl wallcovering lends a shimmering, textured appearance to closet doors in the dressing area of the Master Bath. A swivel stool provides easy access to the convenient built-in drawers and practical counter surfaces.*

Behind a velvet-upholstered sofa in the Master Bedroom is a wall covered with the same fabric and dotted in a regular pattern with small chrome studs. Cantilevered bookshelves, painted the same warm hue, exhibit books and decorative objects, including coral specimens.

STUDIES IN STYLE

Leo Dennis and Jerry Leen, interior designers and antiquarians of impeccable taste, have created a shop in Los Angeles that attracts many customers, including any number of designers. Their collaboration began by accident years ago when they met at a sale at the Santa Barbara Museum of Art. Very soon afterwards they decided to open a shop together. They went to Europe, and spent nine months driving everywhere. "We spent time in museums, where we played a game," says Mr. Dennis. "We pretended we could have anything in the museum we wanted, and we put together imaginary rooms. We could use anything that existed in the world."

When they returned, they opened the shop of Dennis and Leen. They did everything themselves, including covering the walls with rough-hewn redwood, something no one had done in those days. They fabricated an unpretentious background, and then brought in glorious heroic objects and let them speak for themselves. Today the shop is located in an old winery on Robertson Boulevard. Chandeliers from many periods and countries hang from unfinished rafters. On a plaster wall is an oval garden urn looted from Versailles during the French Revolution. There is a rich cornucopia piled on a handsome Chinese lacquered table, and there are eighteenth-century fabrics from Persia, Indonesia and Afghanistan. The two designers have culled the best from all over the world, and they have made a further choice selection for their individual apartments.

As might be expected, Jerry Leen's apartment has no extra line or nuance. It is neither high ceilinged nor architecturally grand. He has, in fact, treated the space with discipline: It is hard, precise, with many fascinations. The apartment is so subtly arranged that its most appealing aspect is a settled quiet. Yet there is a full measure of roughness and complexity to complement the refinement. Royal African grass cloth contrasts with Venetian taffeta; Genoese cut velvet covers an Austrian Baroque chair, its back upholstered in burlap. An elaborate console displays lead and early Ming bronze, antique silver and crystal. A cool elegance is everywhere. "The most marvelous time for me," says Mr. Leen, "is in the evening when I come home and sit looking out at the garden. Many thoughts come to me and my mind is free. There is a tranquillity here that clarifies and washes away all those surface things that are of no great meaning. For me, it is a time of great joy, a time of magic—one in which I delight."

On the other hand, his partner has some rather different ideas. "In the right circumstances," says Leo Dennis, "I'd be ten times more elaborate. I'd like a room all in oak paneling with rock-crystal chandeliers hanging from fifteen-foot ceilings." His own apartment, however, has more conventional eight-foot ceilings. But he displays his favorite objects with robust and generous enjoyment. "I have things here from every part of the world," he goes on, "and I don't play any favorites. It doesn't matter at all to me whether something is old or new, and I don't really care where it comes from. I like furnishings and accessories first for their form, second for their color and third for their quality. I think people make a big mistake in looking only for quality. You can find it, for example, in some big Dutch marquetry cabinet, but it could be hideously ugly. The form is wrong; often the color is bad. In the end, I suppose it simply comes down to a question of taste, to creating some sensible and logical form of décor."

Surely, the work of Mr. Dennis and Mr. Leen demonstrates this sort of taste and logic. With wit and sensitivity they have chosen to appreciate and live with the arts of the whole world.

OPPOSITE: *Eclectic elements blend harmoniously in the Living Room. Appointments include a pair of 17th-century Spanish Colonial gilded stone finials flanking an 18th-century Neapolitan sofa, and two Charles II side chairs — one with cane seat and back and the other upholstered in Royal African grass cloth. A Piranesi water-color of the Roman Coliseum reflects Mr. Leen's antiquarian interests.*
ABOVE LEFT: *Earth tones unify an exotic living room arrangement composed of an African leather bowl filled with ostrich and emu eggs, an 18th-century salt-glazed bear, an American Indian pottery lamp and a pre-Columbian priest's necklace.* BELOW LEFT: *Soft hues distinguish another living room composition, in which a pair of T'ang camels meet before a Duri Amatzu canvas, and a Ming desk frames an ancient vase from Crete.*

LEFT: *Atop an ornate Louis XVI console, a Ming vase filled with spiky branches provides a bold contrast to a pair of gleaming Roman bronzes.* BELOW LEFT: *In a corner of the Bedroom, a calligraphic painting by André Shatu functions as a focal point. An unusual 17th-century ebony and ivory box and an intricate Spanish ivory and tortoise trunk of the same vintage promise hidden mysteries.* OPPOSITE: *Leo Dennis shares his partner Jerry Leen's love of fine objects, and he explains, "I like things first for their form, second for their color and third for their quality." In the Living Room of his Los Angeles apartment, two 18th-century life-size wood figures establish the room's sense of scale. An age-mellowed Samarkand rug serves to unify the space, and a snakeskin walking stick, once used by a maharaja, rests on a concave Egyptian stool.*

Mr. Dennis's Living Room is a treasure
trove of collectibles from every part of
the world. ABOVE LEFT: The carved-wood
pith helmet covered with gold foil belonged
to an Ashanti chieftain. It rests on a
Belgian Louis XVI oak table, with a
Cambodian temple step in the form of a
kneeling goat below. CENTER LEFT: An
Etruscan ivory cup highlights an arrangement that includes a 17th-century
Italian painting. CENTER RIGHT: Shelves
filled with aged parchment books also hold a
collection of small antiquities. BOTTOM LEFT:
A Venetian fresco is a subtle backdrop for
Chinese lotus blossoms and a Han vase.
The William Kent-style console displays
an Etruscan reclining figure and an 11th-
century Persian bowl. The woven-leather
trunk beneath is 19th-century Mexican.

LEFT: *A galloping horse, part of a 17th-century fresco from the ceiling of an Italian palace, animates the Living Room, and a mother-of-pearl Mogul chest gleams in front of the sofa.* BELOW LEFT: *A Chinese portrait and a 17th-century carved-wood shogun on the adjacent terrace bring serenity to the Bedroom. The silk-brocade-covered armchair is Régence. Above the bed is a Louis XIII polychrome cartouche, and on the carpet a French paste dancing slipper whimsically alludes to fairytale heroine Cinderella.*

AN EMPHASIS ON FLEXIBILITY

"Space to me is neither large nor small," says interior designer Tom Allardyce. "That's why I don't create any limitations for myself." Space in this case is his own 950-square-foot apartment, the kind often built in Los Angeles in the late 1930s. Behind grapestake fencing and a small patio is a world removed from the confusions of the city and its shifting values. And it is here that the designer's concepts of style have transcended size and put the lie to what is often considered essential in décor: expensive possessions. "I think of space as a free environment—not as something to hold objects. Today space is at a premium, and we need to do more with less. That's why I prefer to design what goes into the space, or else I'm simply rearranging."

Mr. Allardyce, not content with the usual formulas, has created seating to fit his unique use of space. The size, shape, color and texture of his canvas units can be changed at will. He places cushiony modules against the wall for long, banquettelike seating. He arranges other modules within the high-ceilinged space, singly or in pairs, for conversation areas. When the backs are removed, they become ottomans around a low table. "I start basically with simple materials. I like canvas, and it works well. You see, I think people are coming to an inner awareness of the quality of their lives. What is important to them is what they do, what they accomplish—not what they possess. A fine antique, however, is part of our heritage and should be used, cherished for its art and beauty. But some old pieces are massive, uncomfortable, not easily movable. They have no place in today's life."

Light filters through blinds and casts a soft luster over the room. The walls are clean and bare except for a poetic Rauschenberg. Here and there is the glint of chrome, the shine of glass. Mostly, how-ever, there is light and air and space. Mr. Allardyce would have it no other way. "You walk into a room that is full of objects and fabrics and colors," he says, "and the clutter intrudes on your thinking and feeling. It detracts from your friends. And which come first, people or things?" It is this sort of thinking that he brings to every facet of his design. For example, mirrors used decoratively are often thought to be distractions, but he uses them to create geometric shapes. The reflections form a subtle kaleidoscope of light and shadow, form and texture.

The simplicity of the designer's rooms, like his approach in all areas, reflects a pragmatic attitude rather than a striving for any specific look. There is a small kitchen, however, that seems at first glance an exception, with its display of cooking utensils and baskets. "But everything is here because it has a purpose. It's valid, and there's a function for all these things. That's the important point." It is for the same reason that stereo speakers hang undisguised in the corners of the loft bedroom. "If something has a purpose, I see no need to hide it," the designer explains. "At the moment I'm designing the interiors of an apartment in Hollywood, built forty years ago, with high ceilings, leaded windows and old-fashioned radiators. The radiators will simply be painted the same color as the walls."

Beyond the perceptions of function and comfort, he acknowledges man's need for creativity. There is no more significant catalyst than personal environment, he feels. "When someone walks into this room, he sees a soft, sculptured form that is used for seating. But it doesn't look like a chair in the traditional sense, with two arms and carved legs. He is looking at something in a new way, and that in itself stimulates thought. To me this is as important in design as it is in life itself."

PRECEDING PAGE: *"I think of space as a free environment —not as something to hold objects," says designer Tom Allardyce. His Los Angeles apartment exemplifies this belief: The Living Room, enlivened by a Rauschenberg print, emphasizes functional comfort, not possessions.*

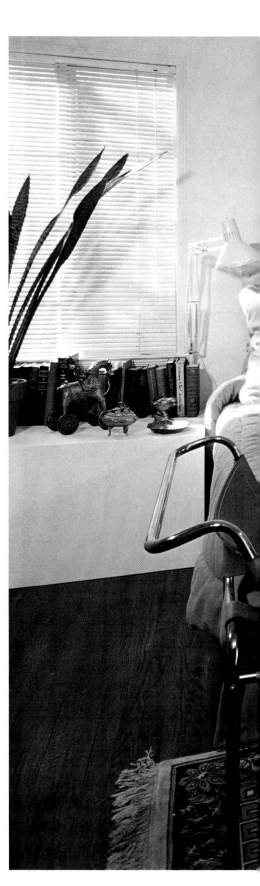

OPPOSITE ABOVE AND BELOW: *In the Living Room, modular canvas-upholstered pillows and a quilted canvas rug reinforce the flexible low-maintenance concept. A mirror adds dimension to the Dining Area, appointed with a glass-topped steel table and bentwood chairs.*

BELOW: *Architecturally enhancing the simplified design, the Bedroom Loft includes a collection of playful pre-Columbian, Siamese and Chinese artifacts. The antique Chinese rug counterpoints sleek modern chairs, functional bedside cubes and a quilted bedcovering.*

SPANISH COLONIAL ECHOES

On the wide and quiet streets of Beverly Hills there are some houses of an undetermined style and age, the kind often built during the 1920s. It was a time when America looked to Europe for guidance in its taste, and travelers tried to duplicate an indiscriminate Mediterranean magnificence at home. Characteristic of the genre is a house built for screen star Norma Talmadge in 1929 that today is the serene residence of Robert Koch Woolf, whose own early background was peopled with the famous of Hollywood. Alongside his father, the noted architect John Woolf, he watched the construction of Hollywood's great houses—those of George Cukor, Fred Astaire, Ira Gershwin, Edgar Bergen, Katharine Hepburn, Bob Hope. And, in those formative years, he also saw the great villas of France, England, Spain and Italy.

Thus, Mr. Woolf is a designer who understands grandeur, but he is also a man of today, who has turned his talents to contemporary living. "I do a good deal of remodeling in this area because there are few spots left to build on, unless you buy an older house and tear it down. But when you take an older house and remodel, it really forces you to think. You have to put it into the correct proportion for a contemporary flow of space; you have to make it function properly." With these thoughts in mind, he restored his present house to its former splendor while bringing it into the contemporary world.

"Someone along the way put in a false ceiling, among other things," he explains. "I imagine it was done in the 1940s for the sake of modernization. Naturally I had it torn out, and what glory is above!" Oxidized by age, the twenty-five-foot-high living room ceiling is dark, its colors recalling the opalescence of the sea. In other ways, because of the designer's work, the house now surpasses itself. He walled in a nondescript fireplace; a living room wall was torn down; and shellstone arches were built to incorporate the gallery—now filled with Pompeiian statues, a T'ang polychrome urn, Louis XIV plaques and the varied forms of many different plants. The living room in particular, permeated with sun and air and fragrance from the garden, imparts a sense of flowing space. Windows are left bare for a view of greenery and flowers. "I could sit out there," says the designer, "and be in the south of France or outside Venice or on a Greek island."

One of the former owners of the house, an actress of some renown, returned to it for one of Mr. Woolf's Christmas parties. She stood at the entrance to the living room and said, "This is exactly the way I wanted this room to look when I lived here. How did you ever manage to do it?" It is, of course, an unanswerable question, since everything depends upon individual circumstances and the designer's approach. "No matter what I'm designing, I don't follow trends. Fads come and go, and I don't pay too much attention to them. I simply do what I think is correct." What is correct for him is a residence with space and proportion, with romance and grandeur, to house the accumulations of a lifetime of collecting.

Everywhere in the house there are treasures from Austria and Germany, from France and Italy and England, from the Orient. "Basically, I'm fondest of the Oriental, although I would not like an all-Oriental house or to have every table painted glass. I admire the way the English use Oriental screens and wallpapers. In fact, the first things I began collecting when I was young were Oriental."

Perhaps Robert Koch Woolf can be called an eighteenth-century man, not in terms of his appreciation for the past alone, but in terms of a tradition reminding us that the finest art of every age remains as timeless as when it was first created.

LEFT: *Weeks were required to cut away the heavy overgrowth of vines that had almost completely covered the exteriors, and years of accumulated paint were sandblasted off the cast-stone walls of the Front Entrance. A pair of ivy trees in antique Italian terra-cotta pots frames the entryway; antique Italian stone figures of Chinese children playing musical instruments are an engaging touch.*

OPPOSITE: *In the Living Room, a Régence fireplace supports the vertical thrust of four Louis XVI overdoor panels. Shuttered French doors contribute to the sense of symmetry, as do a pair of flambé Chinese porcelain dogs that seem to be watching over the Chinese Export collection on the mantel. A Regency backgammon table and painted Venetian armchairs create an inviting game area.*

Other views of the living room accentuate the scope of Mr. Woolf's fine Oriental collectibles. FAR RIGHT TOP: *A lofty plant, an 18th-century Venetian mirror and a Directoire commode set off the display of T'ang and Wei figures. A Hindu temple guard watches nearby.* FAR RIGHT BOTTOM: *Lush velvet-covered pillows counterbalance the delicate clarity of the blanc-de-chine collection and Chinese porcelain lamp on the draped table.*

PRECEDING PAGE: *Built in 1929 for actress Norma Talmadge, the Mediterranean-style Beverly Hills residence of designer Robert Koch Woolf basks in the sun. A view of the Guest House, with its latticed façade and warm stone patio, offers a glimpse of the pool beyond.*

The Dining Room is an arresting blend of Oriental art objects and 18th-century furnishings. A Louis XVI painted marble-topped console presents an array of Ming and Chinese Export porcelains; Chinese wall paintings on glass overlook a sumptuously set Venetian table.

Radiating a rich warmth, the Master Bedroom's bright hues and flowing damask draperies impart an atmosphere of luxury. The cheerily commodious room affords space for a comfortable seating area, as well as a music corner furnished with an 18th-century Austrian Directoire piano that holds a gallery of photographs.

STYLE AND SENSIBILITY

The apartment building in which interior designer Helen Partello lives would be striking in almost any part of the world. It is particularly so in the largely contemporary context of Los Angeles. Hidden among a forest of tall buildings on Wilshire Boulevard, the structure could well be mistaken for some Gothic château in France. Not surprisingly, the designer's small apartment radiates a European sensibility. Walls are highly lacquered; there are dramatic Oriental accents and a number of interesting avant-garde paintings. The international character of the apartment, so characteristic of Helen Partello, symbolizes something of the distance she likes to keep between herself and the large modern city outside.

Although she has lived in this city for a number of years, it is apparent that the designer does not feel herself to be quite a part of it. A few small details here and there — the Louis Vuitton notebook on the desk, the French mustards and Amaretto di Saronno in her kitchen — confirm her cosmopolitan interests. These interests are not at all surprising, of course, since she has lived abroad, spending happy years studying the fine arts in France. She felt little compulsion to study interior design as such. "The creation of décor," she explains, "is not something you can be taught. To my mind, it's simply a matter of taste." And what better cultivation of taste could there be than the study of the fine arts of Europe?

Today she uses her small and elegant apartment as a base, operating what is in essence a one-woman business. More often than not, her clients are in some form associated with the arts. They are writers, collectors, painters, people who are as much at home in one country as another. She has been asked to design the interiors of houses in Aspen, of apartments in New York, of small hotels and private clubs in Europe. The people for whom she designs see a kin-dred spirit in Helen Partello, and they are inclined to give her a free hand, knowing as they do that the results will accurately reflect their own attitudes and preferences. Often her close working relationships with clients develop into enduring friendships.

As the eclectic mixture of furniture and accessories in her own apartment testifies, she is quite at home in any period, from the most traditional to the most contemporary. With apparent ease she is able to duplicate the formal splendors of the eighteenth century or the sleek starkness of modern Italian décor. Why, then, is she not living in New York or London or Paris — cities, as she freely admits, where the stimuli for her visual imagination and the urbane excitement are rather more evident than in Los Angeles? She smiles enigmatically. "Well, I'm not really sure. I *seem* to want to get away, but here I am after all these years. I travel a great deal, so I don't lose touch with other cities and countries. And I will say that in my field it is often easier to accomplish things here in Los Angeles. The pace is not nearly so hectic and confusing as it is in New York, for instance. And there *is* something special here, you know."

To experience the aura of her own apartment is to understand a little more clearly what she means. Los Angeles, with its relatively short history and its face to the future, is after all the ideal setting in which to express an international accent of style. Perhaps *only* in Los Angeles, that most diffuse of all cities, could the echoes of so many different settings harmonize so well, avoiding a clash of temperament with a long-established order. Helen Partello's apartment brings to its surroundings the various feelings of the bustle of New York, the luster of Paris, the elegance of a tree-lined street overlooking Rome's Piazza di Spagna. The striking blend of these differing cultures creates its unique charm.

Contemporary paintings and a Los Angeles location notwithstanding, designer Helen Partello's apartment recalls an earlier, more tranquil age. PRECEDING PAGE: In the Living Room, a 19th-century mirror and a Victorian chimneypiece stand out prominently against lacquered walls. Lending color and pattern are a Persian rug, a Neo-Classical bergère and a 1930s sofa; the Cambodian stupa adds an exotic note. ABOVE AND RIGHT: The living room's vaulted ceiling and mullioned windows provide an architecturally exciting setting for a Regency sofa and a Chinese painted leather chest. OPPOSITE: Dramatized by an antique kilim rug and a dark-toned ceiling, and warmed by chintz-covered walls, the Dining Room doubles as a cozy seating area for after-dinner conversation.

Mirrors reflect and miniaturize the Bedroom's intricate floral wallcovering, creating an intriguing juxtaposition of large and small patterns. Delicate Victorian silver collectibles, telescoping candlestick lamps and two elegant roses adorn the long, draped dressing table.

*Another view of the Bedroom reveals a window curtained
in organdy and draped in the same flowered chintz
that covers a boudoir chair. Framed 18th-century
Chinese embroideries maintain the floral motif, while a
Louis Philippe armoire contributes an air of solidity.*

FOCUS ON DETAIL

"There was a time when I wanted to get rid of everything that had gone before. But at this point in my life, I simply want to explore unfamiliar possibilities."

Interior designer William Gaylord speaks reflectively as he stands before the polished chrome hearth of his San Francisco residence. With its sensuous contrasts of chrome and glass, warm travertine, soft leather and ribbed silk, it seems a brilliant contemporary statement — exactly what might be expected of a designer who considers being "in touch with the times" of first importance.

His home is the upper flat of an 1870 shingled Victorian house high on Russian Hill, with a spectacular view of San Francisco Bay. Inside, however, all historical references vanish. Almost the entire eighteen-hundred-square footage was gutted. "I like to think of myself as an engineer as well as an interior designer," says Mr. Gaylord. "I like to build, rather than simply gather things to fill a space."

Gazing about the large square living room, he points out the balance of the area: a seating group for five in the center facing the fireplace, another seating group for eight at the terrace end, a dining table for eight opposite. "This is a far more classical approach than I have used before. My hope is to achieve some sense of continuity. You can't forget all the things that have gone before." Appropriately enough, he says this from the comfortable depth of a favorite Louis XVI chair, one of two signed originals and two uncannily accurate reproductions — all now upholstered in dark leather that contrasts quite handsomely with the pale leather contemporary setting he designed for the room.

For the designer, this apartment represents a "good deal of where I've been, and the point I've arrived at." Urban, urbane and opulent, it is the summation of a most provocative talent. "I like order and control in design, but form and function are not enough. A room has to have comfort; it has to have a little intrigue; it has to have fantasy and magic. The unexpected is the vital element."

This sense of fantasy can be found in the rounded living room bookshelves that appear suspended in their niche, and were designed to slide into place like drawers. There is also the sense of mystery in the five-hundred-pound steel-and-glass transom that delineates space at the head of the stairs. How did it ever get up there after the wall was upholstered? This is an engineering feat Mr. Gaylord will not reveal. And there is also the baffling feat of the dining table — a slab of marble weighing over half a ton — that could never really rest on that chrome column. The secret is in hidden steel plates and a post anchored beneath the floor itself.

Lighting, too, is an integral part of the fantasy. Although two skylights were introduced to the flat, the rooms are really designed for evening. There is a total of ninety-four ceiling and floor lights designed in sophisticated harmony. All lights are controlled by a master switch, and the entire apartment can be lightened or darkened with one gesture. But, in addition, each room has its own concealed control system. There are nineteen dimmers in the living room alone. In the suede-lined bedroom all daylight can be sealed out with shutters. "I read in bed," says the designer, "so I installed little bullet lights. You push a button, and they hit just the book — not your head or face or knees. Many designers have a tendency to overlook comfort."

Not Mr. Gaylord, however, for he wants to imbue his contemporary design with a quality that still imparts the sensibility of what once was called gracious living. The apartment on Russian Hill is one measure of his success in achieving that goal.

PRECEDING PAGE: *Designer William Gaylord virtually rebuilt the upper flat of an 1870s Victorian house to create his San Francisco residence. The Living Room was originally two small parlors and a porch; only the high Victorian ceiling recalls the former structure.*

LEFT: *Light earth tones prevail in the living room, where warm-hued silk-upholstered walls provide a unifying background for a leather sofa, a table of solid marble sections and geometric-patterned carpeting— all of Mr. Gaylord's own design. A pair of Louis XVI chairs, a Ming vase and a 25th Dynasty Egyptian head add a historical dimension to the predominantly contemporary environment. Highly sophisticated lighting, operated by a control system hidden behind an upholstered panel, allows subtle modulation of the room's atmosphere.* BELOW LEFT: *A fire blazes day and night in the mirror and chrome fireplace. The well-stocked log bin proves the decorative potential of neatly stacked wood.*

"I like to think of myself as an engineer as well as a designer," says William Gaylord. And his residence is filled with proof of his engineering expertise: A non-structural 500-pound transom symbolically divides the Dining Area from the entrance stairway, and a two-inch-thick marble-topped table seems to float upon its 18-inch-diameter chrome base. Surrounding it are Miës van der Rohe chairs; topping it, an unrestrained arrangement of lilies; and as a backdrop, a painting by James Dykes.

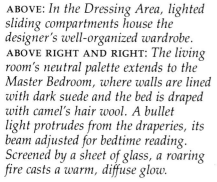

ABOVE: *In the Dressing Area, lighted sliding compartments house the designer's well-organized wardrobe.*
ABOVE RIGHT AND RIGHT: *The living room's neutral palette extends to the Master Bedroom, where walls are lined with dark suede and the bed is draped with camel's hair wool. A bullet light protrudes from the draperies, its beam adjusted for bedtime reading. Screened by a sheet of glass, a roaring fire casts a warm, diffuse glow.*

A contemporary table setting surrounded by sleek modern chairs awaits alfresco diners. The Terrace affords guests a poetic view of the Golden Gate Bridge, spanning San Francisco Bay. Silhouetted against the ebbing glow of the sunset are the dusk-darkened hills of Marin County.

HONORING TRADITION

The area seems more as if it were deep country than Bel-Air in Los Angeles. The hillside, covered with thick vines and shadowed by ancient trees, is broken only by a private road that twists and turns to the top, where a house rests like a pristine retreat, all white against the dark sage of the hill.

The house was built in the 1930s, a time when its view stretched across flatlands unbroken by any building taller than thirteen stories. At night the new street lamps of Wilshire Boulevard could be seen, and Beverly Hills police patrolled around the clock in open Chevrolet touring cars. Since those bygone days few changes had been made on the house until the present owner consulted interior designer William Chidester. "It all started with the garden room," he says. "The room was Colonial, much like the hallway, and very fine. But the owner wanted a more modern room and put up large sheets of mahogany. That's when she called me in and said, 'I see now I've made a terrible mistake.' And I said, 'Don't worry, we can do something about it.' So we added moldings, painted the walls and built in the niches and other details. That was the beginning of major remodeling, and I don't think the owner intended to go as far as she finally did. But she became interested, and she liked what was being done. So one thing led to another, and I was fortunate enough to be able to work closely and effectively with the architect, Mr. Walter Wilkman."

Sliding glass doors were eliminated, rooms extended with bay windows, and an elaborate new wing was built. Today a subdued formality prevails. Fabric upholsters the walls, Oushak rugs cover the dark wood floors and, except in a few instances, light comes from lamps rather than from spotlights. Everywhere there is the warm glow of color, pale and softened. "I like to use color," says the designer.

"I know that many people today are using whites and neutrals, but I think that's just a trend. I've always used color, and I always will."

Mr. Chidester is not concerned with trends. In fact, his approach to design today is much the same as it was when he first started his professional career. "I came to Los Angeles in the 1930s. Nothing was on Robertson Boulevard then. All the design firms were downtown." He worked for Jay Saylor, one of the leading decorators of the day, and went on to become the designer for some of the first families in Southern California. Many are still with him. "I guess they know what to expect. They aren't striving for a particular look or trying to keep up with what's new. My style of designing is not dramatic. I think if I were to give it a name, I would call it 'substantial.' When I design, it's more or less permanent, unless people move or something needs refurbishing. I place great emphasis on quality and detail. I've used the same upholsterers and cabinetmakers for years. I don't shop around for the best price. You can still find excellent craftsmen, but you have to be willing to pay for them."

Recently a great compliment was paid him when a friend of the present owner of the house said, after having spent several hours in the living room, "This room looks as if it's been here forever." It is this feeling of permanence coupled with a careful attention to detail that distinguishes Mr. Chidester's work and endears him to his long-standing clients.

"Nothing is really new," he says. "It's simply a matter of reinterpreting the past in terms of today." He follows this personal credo to the letter, interpreting the past with gentle charm and lively appreciation — continually demonstrating in his special way that the past is not static, but ever changing and open to new translation.

Designer William Chidester gave a colorful new aspect to the interior of a 15-room Georgian Colonial-style residence in Bel-Air. PRECEDING PAGE: *Leafy tree boughs, a winding brick drive and landscape architect Joseph Copp's discriminating arrangement of potted plants, flowers and shrubbery soften the dignified columned exterior.* RIGHT: *In the Garden Room, warm hues function as a lively background for an extensive art collection, including a Chinese spinach jade carving on the coromandel-topped table and a Daumier bronze silhouetted against the window. Nearby, a William Chase portrait, a Louis Valtat still life and a T'ang glazed pottery horse further animate the setting. The blend of grace and solidity is underscored by an Oushak rug.*

A Matisse bronze sculpture of a girl leaning on a fence is the focal point of another comfortable seating arrangement in the Garden Room. Gleaming atop a nearby commode, a sleek gilded bronze Carbonel figure shares the spotlight with a painting by Jean-Baptiste Ange Tissier.

Handpainted Chinese wallpaper and crystal chandelier and candelabra brighten the Dining Room. In contrast, the burled walnut table, English buffet and parquet flooring sound a deeper note. The table setting includes Imari porcelains precisely placed on lacquer trays.

At one end of the Living Room, Chinese porcelains, bergères covered in embroidered silk, flowered pillows and an Oushak rug offer a harmony of patterns; even the Heilbuth portrait displays a pattern-filled background to offset its demurely proper subject.

Sunlight streaming into the Living Room through the large bay window illuminates a Louis XVI bureau plat topped with ivories, a miniature chest and a bouillotte lamp, and adds a dappled pattern to the parquet floor. The Louis XV cane-backed desk chair is signed Remy.

OPPOSITE, LEFT AND RIGHT: *Renoir's portrait of his son, above the Louis XV mantel, dominates another commodious living room grouping that includes Louis XV bergères. Across the room, a Louis XV chinoiserie lacquer secrétaire adds a balancing counterpoint.*

BELOW: *Bright pastels suffuse the Master Bedroom with good cheer, and a spacious sitting area is arranged invitingly around a crackling fire. A collection of Chinese porcelain adorns the Louis XVI mantel; the Marie Laurencin painting of a girl suits the room's overall delicacy.*

ABOVE: *A reclining nude by Moïse Kisling adds a sensuous note to the wood-paneled Guest Bath.* BELOW RIGHT: *In the Master Bath, a Hereke silk prayer rug warms marble flooring. A variety of potted plants, an Italian stone amore and a Chinese porcelain pillow in the form of a kneeling figure reinforce the decorative effect of wooden moldings and window shutters. The Louis XV slipper chair and stool upholstered in matching floral fabric echo the rosy hues of the stately orchids. Satisfying the need for privacy, outdoor greenery provides a natural screen and a restful view for bathtime contemplation.*

Flowered chintz lends a springtime air to the Master Bedroom's window draperies, Louis XVI-style canopy bed and Louis XV slipper chair. Small sofa pillows and the handmade Spanish rug resound with floral overtones. Meissen mandarins grace a Korean lacquer table.

LEFT: *Pots of flowers ranged in orderly progression mount the brick stairway leading from a poolside terrace to the garden's iron gazebo. Half-hidden stone figures peer from the dense surrounding foliage, and well-established trees and ferns reach upward toward the clear sky.* ABOVE: *A small West African sculpture serves as sentinel, standing guard at the sliding glass door that opens from the Garden Room to the terrace beyond.* BELOW: *Outside the garden room, a placid tree-surrounded pool awaits swimmers. Flowers and tall shrubs in latticed planters add detail, and a crowing rooster proudly puffs his sculptured plumage.*

CONTEMPORARY CLARITY

It is an area in Los Angeles known as the Outpost Estates, a name suitable for the setting and terrain, but something of a misnomer as to location, since five minutes below the scrub-covered hills and deep canyons are rows of anonymous apartment buildings. In spirit, however, Outpost is far from the city and attracts those whose interests in the expression of individuality are as important to their lives as any consideration of space and privacy.

One residence here—its conventional exterior giving little hint as to its interior design—shows a remarkable use of space. The rooms, built high over the ground, give the illusion of floating far up in the sky. "As with any interior," says designer Ray Gray, "space must be realized first. I take out all the things I feel are unnecessary." Walls, banisters and what he refers to as "ruffles" were removed, and small areas were reshuffled. Ceilings were dropped to make a space intimate or raised to align with an adjoining room. He removed doors and extended entrances from the standard three-foot width to four. Walls were enlarged to appear thicker and to suggest "those wonderful heavy stone entranceways that are often seen in certain parts of Greece."

Now clean-swept and simplified, the rooms nonetheless contain a complexity of styles. There are rich borrowings from Art Déco, from the form and function of the Bauhaus and from the civilization of Crete. "The hardest thing about collecting," says Mr. Gray, "is to arrange everything so that a room doesn't have a specific period look. And it's easy to fall into the trap of clutter and put everything out. Then you're tripping over things all the time."

His way is completely different. There are few fabrics and no prints. Blinds regulate the light, taming it in summer, intensifying it during the winter months. There are very few keepsakes. Mermaid figures from an Italian ocean liner of the 1930s rise into the space. Plaques from an MGM Persian epic decorate one wall. What few artifacts there are have personal significance to the owners of the house.

"They have no help in the house," the designer explains. "If you have a lot of artifacts, then you need to give a lot of elaborate instructions as to their care." However, it is a formal house, not at all in a punctilious way, but rather in its fastidiousness of thought. The clean realism shuns the sentimentality sometimes found in a more antique décor. There is neither a cloying ruffle nor a piece of wallpaper. In every real sense it is an enlightened space.

The designer is attracted to the Pop Art way of thinking, and one kitchen cabinet is painted with a milk company logo. "In a funny way I intended the design as a backdrop for flights of fancy. I like a house where people laugh, where they are completely liberated." The bedroom, for example—which contains only a bed, two lamps and a sculpture stand serving as a chest of drawers—is, according to Mr. Gray, one of the most perfect rooms in the house: "It is completely functional and unrestricted," he says, "even down to the color, which is no color."

Simplicity extends to the garden, where a Schiaparelli mirror reflects staghorn ferns and a view of rolling brown hills. The original garden, bushy with daisies and roses, gave way to geometric cacti and succulents. It is a garden of grays, sparse and windswept. A late evening breeze blows from the hills, and there is a feeling of isolation from the manmade brilliance that glows in the distance.

When compared with the art of Europe, there is much in the house that is primitive. But it is also a reminder that when the primitive is combined with luxury, the end result is luxury raised to its highest and most provocative power.

The Art Déco mood throughout this Los Angeles residence was conceived by interior designer Ray Gray. PRECEDING PAGE: *In the Living Room, a statue by Libero Andreotti, commissioned in 1931 for the liner* Victoria, *mirrors similar figures in a painting by Bodhi Wind.*

Low marble tables surrounded by alpaca-upholstered
chairs emphasize the glowing warmth of the Living
Room. A cluster of vases and a bronze head by Kélèty are
poised on one table; a lamp by Gae Aulenti and a botan-
ical arrangement in a graceful vase are arresting details.

ABOVE: *A Jacques Schnier plaque, created for the 1939
Golden Gate International Exposition in San Francisco,
stands out brilliantly against the Dining Room
wallcovering.* RIGHT: *The sweeping lines of an
Achaemenian-style bas-relief acquired from Metro
Goldwyn Mayer echo the more subtle curves of the
1938 game table and chairs in the Entrance Hall.*

The Master Bedroom's monochromatic background
and spare furnishings achieve a feeling of space and
purity. A pair of glowing Italian lamps highlights a
majestic sculpture stand that ingeniously conceals a
chest of drawers. Surmounting it are a Japanese
lacquered wood figure and a gilt Chinese wood
sculpture, both dating from the 19th century.

SAN FRANCISCO CADENCE

"I found the house," says interior designer Val Arnold. "I saw it, and twenty minutes later I called my client and said, 'You're going to buy a house today.' She said that was impossible. But she came down, and bought it immediately. Even the realtor didn't understand. No one could see the potential."

Thus Mr. Arnold describes the start of the redesign of an erstwhile brick firehouse in San Francisco's Pacific Heights, which he groomed into an Italianate beauty for a third-generation native of San Francisco who is also a dear friend. The building had originally been converted to a residence in 1925, and over the years the interior was subjected to some rather unfortunate modernization. Nevertheless, as Val Arnold notes, the floor plan was very good, the rooms had fine proportions and, extraordinary for hilly San Francisco, there was access to a level terrace from the living room, the dining room and the all-purpose room near the kitchen.

It was this terraced garden, on view and accessible from all the downstairs rooms, that made the house so special. And the special house became, in the designer's word, "phenomenal" when they added a swimming pool at the bottom of the sun-drenched and tree-screened garden. Completely sheltered from the winds that normally make an outdoor pool impractical in San Francisco, the garden is a singular retreat from the city.

In the garden, or looking out on it from downstairs or upstairs, there are no clues to the locale. It could be a beautiful sunny garden anywhere the terrain requires stepped terraces. But within the house there is a persistent sense of place. A feeling of northern Italy — something of Tuscany, something of Venice — pervades the dining room and is even more evident elsewhere. Just how this ambience is achieved is a mystery, for Italian antiques are mingled with old family pieces of English and French pedigree and exquisite examples of Orientalia, from fine Chinese snuff bottles to an Imari vase that inspired the coloration of the master suite.

The interior design began with a treasure hunt that yielded some prize finds. Just before work on the house commenced, the owner inherited an estate that included the entire contents of a venerable San Francisco mansion. "We went to the house," says Mr. Arnold, "and it was like Christmas. I insisted that we go through every box, every barrel, every cupboard." Their finds were rich ones: a pair of plaques that turned out to be rare Sèvres; a traveling case with eighteen-karat gold fittings; a coromandel screen; and all the inviting old upholstered pieces now rehabilitated and incorporated into the living room décor. But Val Arnold is an architectural designer, whose décor begins with the basics; so after the treasure hunt was completed a year of painstaking work with contractors began.

"I try to see the architectural content of a room first," he says, describing himself as "a comfort creature." So creature comforts are the key to the architectural changes on the upper floor, where he juggled spatial elements. For instance, by eliminating one small bedroom, he enlarged the master suite to include a dressing room/bath. Such changes provide welcome continuity to the house, a continuity that is enhanced by the colors reiterated from room to room — sometimes strongly, sometimes in pale shades — but never precisely duplicated.

"I try to key a house to a certain specific accent color that somehow goes into every room in some small quantity." So, with scale, proportion and color modulation, Val Arnold has provided a cohesiveness that goes beyond room-to-room décor into an evocative statement of personality.

PRECEDING PAGE: *An Italianate grace and the glow of rich
color suffuse the Living Room
of an unusual San Francisco
home designed by Val Arnold.*

BELOW: *Active patterns and restful solids contribute to
the living room's lively aspect. Framed Indian
miniatures, jewellike, complement the intricacy of an
18th-century Dutch bombé secretary, a 19th-century
Spanish rug and Italian columns used as plant stands.*

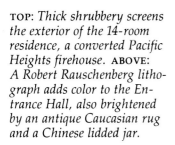

TOP: *Thick shrubbery screens
the exterior of the 14-room
residence, a converted Pacific
Heights firehouse.* ABOVE:
*A Robert Rauschenberg litho-
graph adds color to the Entrance Hall, also brightened
by an antique Caucasian rug
and a Chinese lidded jar.*

OPPOSITE BELOW: *A coromandel screen, behind an ornately carved 17th-century gilt console, lends its complex imagery to a corner of the Living Room. Delicate blossoms in an antique Chinese jardinière add another Oriental touch to the predominantly Italian mood.*

BELOW: *Stalwart 19th-century leather-upholstered chairs attend a Parsons table in the warm-hued Dining Room, where shuttered windows and French doors afford an inviting view of the sun-drenched terraced garden. An ornate Venetian-style chandelier is a graceful accent.*

BELOW: *Like summer gardens blossoming in a field of snow, flower-strewn bedcovers adorn a pair of antique Spanish four-poster beds, with intricately wrought headboards, in the Guest Room. Carpeting of Brussels velvet enhances the pervasive feeling of serenity.*

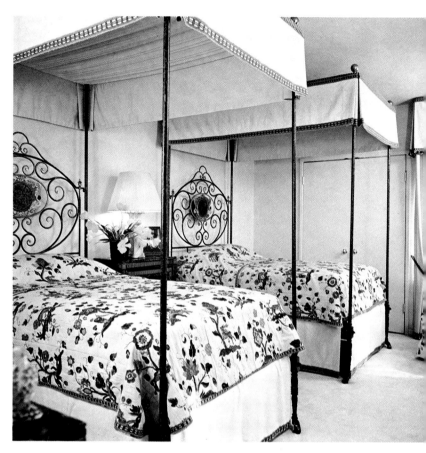

ABOVE LEFT AND LEFT: *The Master Bedroom is doubly indebted to the Orient: Not only does an Imari lamp illuminate a desk displaying a pair of miniature family portraits, but the draperies also borrow their color and design from this much-loved Japanese porcelain.*

Warm color notes accent the Master Bedroom's bright airiness. The 19th-century French lacquer desk is well situated to take full advantage of the sunlight. An arrangement of orchids is a delicate foil to the nostalgic presence of a sturdy antique Franklin stove.

BELOW: *The freshly planted and flagstone-paved Garden is accessible from all the downstairs rooms — a luxury that is quite a rarity in hilly San Francisco. Terraces, vibrant with colorful flowers and budding trees, provide a succession of restful refuges from the bustle of the city.*

RIGHT: *Sheltered by trees from the blustery bay winds, a pool of azure beauty sits at the lowest level of the garden. Beside it a glass-topped table, already set for an outdoor luncheon, awaits guests. The love of flowers evident throughout the interior here gains its fullest expression.*

ELEGANCE FOR A WORKING RANCH

"If I have any one philosophy of design," says Mrs. Frank S. Wyle, "it is that structure must come out of environment." She is speaking about a weekend house she and her husband built on their working Black Angus cattle ranch in North Fork, California. The ranch and the house itself are situated on three thousand acres of meadowland and mountain terrain some thirty miles north of Fresno.

"We've had the land since 1959 and have added parcels to it over the years. For me this ranch typifies the real California—the way it used to be. When we finally decided to build," she continues, "there was no question about where to put the house. We went to the spot instantly, though we had many acres to choose from." There was a profusion of redbud, and a lovely stream meandered through the site. Their decision proved to be practical as well as aesthetic. At the suggestion of their architect, John Rex, the Wyles camped out on the chosen site in a trailer, "to be absolutely certain." A year passed, and they had channeled the stream into a small lake. They were ready to build. At first they planned only a small cabin, but a three-story house soon emerged. "I'm very happy it worked out that way," says Mrs. Wyle. "The house is now in perfect proportion to its surroundings." Its pure, sturdy lines—the stonework pylons, in particular—resemble the Japanese buildings she and her husband so admire. In fact, they had brought back photographs of Osaka Palace from the Orient and given them to Mr. Rex.

"I don't think I've ever designed a more successful indoor and outdoor house," says the architect. Basically, the structure is an open pavilion that conveys a feeling of space and freedom, quite in harmony with its environment. And for the interior, Mrs. Wyle, herself a painter for many years, insisted on using natural materials and earth tones to complement the exterior. Care was taken to see that all materials, whenever possible, came from North Fork itself in order to emphasize the house's remarkable affinity with the natural scene. Granite for the stonework was quarried right on the ranch. The pavilion columns are Douglas fir; the sidings, western red cedar; and the interior flooring, wide white oak stained a tawny brown-black, suggesting the bark on the pine trees. Inside the house couches are covered in material carefully chosen to match the color of a lichen that proliferates on the ranch.

"The important thing was not to compete with the scenery," explains Mrs. Wyle. "My husband and I chose the California designer Sam Maloof to create the furniture. His style is pure and clean. I like to think of it as contemporary Shaker. He makes each piece himself, and the finished product is like sculpture to see and touch." Mr. Maloof designed the walnut pieces for the house with a larger-than-usual horizontal base to counter the vertical form of the building itself. Sturdy cedar-and-leather outdoor chairs from San Miguel de Allende complement these designs, as do antique wooden chests from New Mexico. To emphasize the simplicity and natural feeling of the interiors, Mrs. Wyle has hung very few paintings; the most striking wall decoration is an antique Navajo rug in the bedroom. All the textiles used in the house continue the natural theme, and they come from every part of the world. Every piece is handwoven: the Polish goat-hair rug in front of the fireplace, the natural wool rug from Yugoslavia, the smaller Moroccan rugs that are placed under chairs and by the stairwell.

The Wyles' residence in Los Angeles is also filled with beautiful objects, but they prefer the ranch. "We exist in town," says Mrs. Wyle, "but we *live* in North Fork, surrounded by the wonders of nature."

PRECEDING PAGE: *Three thousand acres of meadow and mountain terrain surround Edith and Frank Wyle's weekend retreat, a working Black Angus cattle ranch in North Fork. A profusion of redbud trees and a meandering stream determined their choice of building site; architect John Rex took advantage of the spot's seclusion to design an open, pavilionlike structure, primarily of glass.*

LEFT: *On three sides, a cantilevered redwood deck 7½ feet deep thrusts the house into the environment. Cedar-and-leather chairs from San Miguel de Allende extend the use of natural materials, while a pottery bird feeder by Pat Casad and an East Indian parasol add gentle whimsy to the outdoor décor.* OPPOSITE: *One of the umbrellalike modules supporting the roof of the house is evident in this view of the Living Area and the peaceful pond it overlooks.*

The owners' insistence on the use of local materials strengthens the structure's link with its surroundings: Behind the fireplace in the Living Area's conversation pit, a pylon made of granite quarried on the ranch brings the grandeur of nature indoors.

RIGHT: *For the conversation pit couches Edith Wyle chose a fabric to match the color of a lichen that proliferates on the ranch. Handloomed textiles collected in Switzerland, Peru and Poland cover the pillows. The handwoven goat-hair rug also comes from Poland, and the basket in the foreground is Hopi. The iron staircase beyond leads to the gallery and bedrooms.*

RIGHT: *In the Dining Area, the table, benches and chairs, designed by Sam Maloof, have a sculptural purity reminiscent of Shaker furniture. Carol Funai's pottery bowl, filled with wild flowers gathered from the ranch, blends with the subtle variations of color in the wood grain.*

THE CHANDLER HOUSE

When Mrs. Norman Chandler decided it was time to refurbish her house in an old, well-established area of Los Angeles, she immediately called upon interior designer Leonard Stanley. The driving force behind the creation of the Music Center, which has done much to revitalize downtown Los Angeles, she had worked closely with Mr. Stanley on the interiors of that cultural complex. Mrs. Chandler was most familiar with his approach to décor since they had developed great rapport and mutual respect during the planning and execution of the cultural center. Leonard Stanley speaks of her with the admiration of a professional designer, saying, "She never changed her mind after making a decision."

Because Mrs. Chandler's days are so active and her schedule so crowded, she felt it particularly important for her home to maintain a serene atmosphere and offer a restful escape from the pressures of the outside world. In refurbishing the house, she sought a new look, yet she wanted to have favorite objects and furnishings surrounding her. Being so familiar with Leonard Stanley's work, she was certain that he could refresh and rearrange her home without sacrificing any of its traditional character. Though Mr. Stanley's own preferences run to eventful interiors and an often iconoclastic approach, he has the professional integrity that places the needs and wishes of his clients first. Naturally, he saw his role with clarity. His task was to create a background that reflected Mrs. Chandler, not himself. "I don't like anything that really looks 'decorated,'" he says. "And I don't like anything that can be identified immediately with the work of a particular designer. If, in the end, my personality comes to dominate an interior, I can only say that I have not been successful. That sort of domination does not, in my opinion, lie in the realm of the designer. It is occasionally true, however, that one will find a client with no special personality of his or her own to express. Nevertheless, it doesn't happen very often, and it certainly didn't happen in the case of Mrs. Chandler. She is a true individualist, with ideas of her own and with excellent taste to match."

The question of taste is an interesting and provocative one; Mr. Stanley feels that everyone has it to one degree or another. Taste, however, as both he and Mrs. Chandler fully understand, has very little to do with the trends of the moment. "I don't believe in rushing out and buying a fabric, or anything else," the designer explains, "simply because it's in style at the time. It's costly to decorate and wasteful to redo your house every time some new trend appears. Good décor—and I'm sure that Mrs. Chandler would agree—does not go out of style."

Built in 1913, her house is in the grand manner of the turn of the century. "It functions now almost exactly as it was originally meant to," says Mr. Stanley. "There are the servants, the rooms for china and silver, the enormous kitchen. For Mrs. Chandler has always entertained extensively, and people come to her house from all over the world." The fact that the designer was so familiar with her way of life, coupled with his own knowledge of and fondness for traditional elegance, contributed a great deal to his successful revitalizing of the Chandler residence.

However, possibly the strongest link between Mrs. Chandler and her interior designer was their mutual respect for quality. It was a subject they often discussed, trying to decide whether styles of one period are superior to those of another. Together they came to the conclusion that quality is the common denominator that marks the best décor of any period. "And quality," says Mr. Stanley, "is something Mrs. Chandler understands extremely well."

A traditional grace pervades Mr. and Mrs. Norman Chandler's Los Angeles home, which they invited designer Leonard Stanley to redecorate for them. PRECEDING PAGE: *Period furnishings and an Aubusson rug give the Music Room a European air.*

BELOW: *Demilune windows admit soft light into the Library, where a Picasso portrait is a striking note above a Georgian-style chimneypiece. European and Chinese Export porcelains create background detail for English tables and chairs, and sofas upholstered in floral fabric.*

BELOW AND BOTTOM: *Travertine walls—one curved and adorned with a panoramic mural—marbleized columns and a great stretch of window enhance the Loggia. Chandeliers, a central table, an ornate mirror and the console beneath it establish the room's axis.*

OPPOSITE: *A lively floral chintz, a Victorian chandelier and baskets brimming with plants and flowers lend an inviting aspect to a Guest Room. Within this cozy retreat, an English four-poster bed, surmounted by a graceful canopy, adds the element of individuality.*

ABOVE: *Light-hued formality suffuses the Dining Room, where silk taffeta draperies create a pattern of soft folds that restate the linear motif of gilt-edged boiserie. Louis XV table and chairs, large Chinese vases and a delicate Savonnerie rug augment the harmonious blend of comfort and sumptuousness.* RIGHT: *An intricate iron gate and a fountain offset an orderly bed of flowers in the Garden. Sunlight filtered through tall trees washes walls and paths with free-form shadows.*

ELAN IN LOS ANGELES

As Los Angeles interior designer J. P. Mathieu sees it, the common denominator in his field of endeavor is to be found in the one word *style*. It is a word open to many interpretations, and Mr. Mathieu is secure enough to illustrate it not only in the fabrics and furniture he designs for his showrooms in Los Angeles and Miami, but in the Los Angeles apartment he created for his own use as well.

"To be honest, I don't like the decorated look. If I work on your house, for example, I want to leave the impression that you did it all yourself—that there really wasn't a decorator involved." He looks around his apartment with a smile. "Well, at least that's what I tried to do *here*." The result is not quite as ingenuous as it sounds, and Mr. Mathieu had some important advantages from the beginning. He lives in an older building with many generous architectural details, and he did not have to compensate for the sterile divisions of space that mark a good deal of modern construction. His apartment has high ceilings, beautiful wood floors, large windows and an unusual floor plan. He has fulfilled the potential of this space with a rich mixture of his own.

"In recent years," he explains, "both decorators and clients have become far more knowledgeable and sophisticated. We have finally reached a point where we can mix different periods with confidence." The mixture he uses for himself is catholic: eighteenth-century Italian provincial, Art Déco, Ch'ien Lung porcelain, Japanese lacquer, Philippine straw baskets, Indian fabrics, Moroccan tables, Oriental rugs, seventeenth-century Spanish polychrome angels. The mixture is elaborate, but nothing is overpowering, nothing out of place. Still, the apartment is by no means an exercise in understatement; rather, it demonstrates careful control. Take, for example, the vibrant silk panel from the Peking Opera Company, used so effectively in the living room. It is an object entirely capable of overwhelming an ordinary room, or leading to decorative excesses. But Mr. Mathieu, while surely exploiting the panel's dramatic effect, has softened its impact by centering furniture of his own design in front of it. The sofa, chairs and ottoman are simple and neutral. "But I do like to create a bit of fantasy once in a while. I might even change the décor when I'm giving a dinner party in order to add some drama. Mood is very important to me."

The occasional fantasy and bold statement apart, Mr. Mathieu is content to devote his life and his designs to simplicity and understatement. These qualities have made him much in demand, and he spends a lot of time working on projects, both commercial and residential, in many parts of the world.

The people for whom he works appreciate his insistence on quality; they also value his realism. When he takes on a residential assignment, he does not insist on throwing everything away and making a fresh start. Such an approach, he says, is all too common in the field of decoration. He feels that too many designers tend to be autocratic. The tendency is understandable, but far from desirable. "I know there are decorators with large egos," says Mr. Mathieu, "and they have spoiled many things for the rest of us. I'm not saying that I don't have an ego. But I also have a responsibility to those who pay for my advice. I use what talents I have, and I do make a point of searching out simplicity and style. That's the important thing to maintain—style."

Whether in his own apartment or in a client's house, he prefers to use a simple and beautiful object rather than something merely expensive or ostentatious. Better a handsome straw basket, he feels, than some dubiously elaborate silver bowl.

ABOVE: *Counterpointing a cluster of vertical elements, a Ch'ien Lung porcelain headrest kneels near a Siamese Buddha hand. The well-orchestrated grouping of textures includes hardy wicker, brilliant crystal and delicate porcelain.*
LEFT: *Deep tones and lush plants imbue the Dining Room with a junglelike atmosphere. A Nepalese gold-leafed Buddha hand and a Chinese painting bring a Far Eastern flavor to the scene.*

LEFT: *A pair of Chinese porcelain birds perch on a lacquer tray table in the Sunroom. Plump sofa pillows covered in brightly patterned antique fabrics from Indonesia and India add to the room's allure.*

The Master Bedroom extends the Eastern theme of the residence: A Chinese painting overlooks a table adorned with a collection of sang de boeuf Chinese porcelains and an exotic Indian print wraps the bed. A colonial wooden adoration figure hovers over the scene.

BEVERLY HILLS CHARM

"I hate ruffles and bows and gingham gewgaws, and I loathe four-poster beds with chichi draperies. They're as chilling as a slumber room in a mortuary," says Jean Howard, whose charming and traditionally appointed house has long attracted the beau monde of California's Beverly Hills.

Born in Texas, Jean Howard appeared in the Ziegfeld Follies with such stars as Virginia Bruce and Gypsy Rose Lee; became the confidante of Linda and Cole Porter and of Noel Coward; and photographed many Hollywood notables during the 1940s and 1950s, when she was married to the late entrepreneur Charles Feldman. She is married now to classical guitarist Tony Santoro.

"I like people to come into my living room and not be afraid to sit down," she says. "That's why my taste runs to large pieces of furniture. They're practical and comfortable—I dislike those miniscule French tables with spindly legs that fall over when you take a deep breath. Frankly, I don't care if they *are* $40,000 antiques from Marie Antoinette's bedroom. Linda Porter taught me many things, and it was she who suggested I cover my tables with glass so that you can put down a drink without being afraid of damaging the veneer. Any taste I have about houses, and living, was inspired by Linda. I met the Cole Porters in 1931, when I was sixteen; I adored them, and they adored me. In fact, we really adopted one another, and they generously invited me to all of their wonderful parties.

"Elsie de Wolfe, a most innovative designer and hostess, also taught me a great many things. For example, she was one of the first to insist that the floral centerpiece on a dining room table should be low so that one could talk to the other guests without having to peer through a forest of greenery. In addition to learning from women like Linda Porter and Elsie de Wolfe, I've found out a good deal on my travels. I've found my paintings and furniture and coromandel screens in every part of the world."

Jean Howard points out that the late interior designer William Haines first worked on the décor of her Beverly Hills house. "Perhaps you can say that his work has been slightly updated by the owner," she says smiling, "but Vincent Fourcade and Robert Denning did help a good deal. For example, they chose the patterned carpet in the living room that manages to pull everything together." She is remarkably casual about her collection of paintings and fine porcelain. In the living room there is a good deal of rose-colored Meissen that was left to her by Cole Porter. For dinner parties, she delights in mixing the antique Meissen with modern hammered aluminum plates from Mexico.

"Frankly," says Miss Howard, "this house is for parties. It loves people and good times, and I like to entertain several times a month. At one time or another almost everyone's been here—from Judy Garland and Richard Burton singing their hearts out around the grand piano, to President Kennedy, who loved coming back here for luncheons and dinners."

As a hostess, Jean Howard believes that if one invites beautiful women and attractive men—whether in business, philanthropy or the arts—one has most of the ingredients for a perfect party. And it is her attention to detail and her overwhelming concern for the comfort of her guests that for thirty-six years have made Jean Howard's house a stopping-off place for friends from all over the world. Indeed, it shares with all eminent houses an international air. The house could be anywhere in the world: Paris, Rome, Mexico City, Manhattan—wherever the sophisticated and the accomplished gather together to exchange memories and new ideas.

Jean Howard's fondness for entertaining makes comfort the most important ingredient in her traditionally appointed Beverly Hills home. PRECEDING PAGE: *Complemented by a serene Modigliani portrait, European and Oriental antiques mingle in the Living Room.*

OPPOSITE: *An unusual arrangement of seating groups opens the center of the Living Room, disclosing a fireplace surrounded by beveled mirrors. A Meissen parrot perches on a bronze ring, while Jules Pascin's poetic painting* The Model *seems to bask in the room's radiance.*

ABOVE: *Varied aesthetic traditions coexist harmoniously in a living room niche in which an 18th-century Siamese Buddha is backdropped by Pascin's* Jeune Fille. *A long sofa upholstered in chenille and chairs covered in a chinoiserie glazed chintz offer commodious seating around a table displaying a Berrocal bronze and a tomato-shaped Chinese bowl. Carved pine moldings and densely patterned carpeting provide unifying details.*

OPPOSITE AND BELOW: *Warm-hued and softly illumi-*
nated, the Dining Room is aglow; an 18th-century
Japanese screen with crane motif evokes a sense of
Oriental fantasy. The Irish Georgian table gleams with a
sumptuous setting of silver, crystal and fine porcelain.

FOLLOWING PAGES: *A scenic Japanese screen hanging*
over the bed brings Eastern enchantment to a bowerlike
Bedroom, whose every surface seems strewn with
flowers. Upholstery fabric, wallcoverings, bed linens
and carpeting all are figured in floral motifs, as is the
Chinese red lacquer screen softening a corner. Above it,
Bombois's painting entitled Bowl of Roses *gives an*
artist's interpretation of the room's dominant theme,
while lovely bouquets of real flowers, gathered in the
owner's garden, provide the added beauty of fragrance.

LIGHT AND REFLECTIONS

It is only natural that artist Kalef Alaton, now an interior designer, has approached the complete redesign of a house high in a lovely section of Beverly Hills with a painterly eye. Stone lions, along with clay pots and baskets, are reflected by well-positioned mirrors. Plump sofas and chairs echo the subtle colors of lacquered grasscloth wallcoverings.

"It all started with the Italian panels that are now the front doors," says Mr. Alaton. "The art and design evolved from there." His partner, Janet Polizzi, agrees. From the project's beginning the two designers searched abroad and in the United States for the countless pieces and bibelots necessary to furnish the house. The result is an enclave of treasures: Greco-Roman artifacts, a classic nineteenth-century painting of an odalisque, an Oriental rug placed just below a massive marble hearth.

"The rooms have a Renaissance feeling," says Mr. Alaton, "but very much simplified. We have made no overall theme. Some of the tables are Oriental, as is the living room rug. The mother-of-pearl peacock on the bar is from India. The ornate entry columns and other artifacts originated in Greece or Rome, but they were found in many different places."

Naturally, art figures prominently in the work of the two designers and their client, but it must meet exacting standards. "We are interested in quality," they agree. "The pieces must be good." For example, a vitrine housing some of the owner's artifacts is identical to two that stand behind the desk of President Valéry Giscard d'Estaing in the Elysée Palace in Paris. The mosaic in the hall, discovered in England, turned out to be a very rare and ancient artwork. "Before buying each piece, we consulted with the owner," explains Mr. Alaton. "There were countless phone calls from New York, Europe — wherever we happened to be searching."

The house is flexible. It changes moods hourly, with the lighting. The owner entertains frequently, with intimate dinner parties or more formal soirées for a larger number of friends. And the lighting at night serves to create a perfect party setting. For a change of pace, there is always the side garden, or the pool and adjoining garden.

"The dining room is really my favorite room," says Mr. Alaton. "The Waterford chandelier is replenished daily with candles, and it casts that wonderfully romantic and appealing glow.

"Each of our designs is treated individually, and we avoid trends. I don't think this house will be dated in ten years. The fabrics and colors may be refurbished or changed, but the major effects will remain. The personality of the owner and the design mood should take care of that. Each project we do — traditional or contemporary — has to be different, unique and absolutely unstylized.

"Working with people who have a strong sense of taste, people who know what they want — like the owner of this house — can be tremendously rewarding. And it can also be quite frustrating. I'm sure that my partner also finds this to be true."

The mirrors, the far-reaching view of the city lights and the eclectic array of appointments give a touch of infinity to this house in Beverly Hills. Mirrors in the entrance hall and the living room reflect the art and the many fascinating objects visible on all sides. Despite the museum-quality art and the rare pieces scattered throughout the house, it exudes a feeling of genuine warmth. This is a home to be lived in, and even more, one to be enjoyed.

"One of my favorite times is sunset," says Kalef Alaton. "Then the house, the colors, the furnishings all come alive with a definite sort of magic — almost the magic of a glorious sunset in Greece."

Subtle lighting and a generosity of scale contribute a simplified elegance to a Beverly Hills home designed by Kalef Alaton and Janet Polizzi. OPENING PAGE: George II columns frame the gracious Foyer, where an 18th-century marble amphora strikes the first of many classical chords. PRECEDING PAGES: A marble lion is the salient presence in a section of the Living Room backdropped by a curving wall of glass.

TOP, ABOVE RIGHT AND BELOW RIGHT: In the living room, the symmetrical rhythm of paired appointments is offset by the slightly angled placement of a 19th-century Sultanabad rug. Within this balanced setting, plump upholstered chairs and floor pillows ensure comfort and flexibility. An odalisque by Fernand Cormon hangs on one side of the doorway to the dining room, and a Louis XIV-style Boulle cabinet housing numerous ancient artifacts is on the other.

OPPOSITE: An antique Waterford chandelier — constantly supplied with fresh candles — casts a gentle half-light over the Dining Room table set with a rare and distinctive centerpiece of Phoenician jars and luminous crystal spheres.

LEFT: *An 18th-century chinoiserie lacquer secrétaire establishes a quiet work area in a corner of the Master Bedroom; for moments of relaxation, there is a pillowed chaise longue upholstered in floral-patterned French silk. The curved glass wall admits a garden view.* BELOW LEFT: *A faceted mirror connects the tub with the ceiling well in the Master Bath, where a tiny Brighton Pavilion chair serves as a novel towel stand.* OPPOSITE: *A pastel carpet and pastel walls provide a soft roseate background in the master bedroom. Pairs of English chinoiserie night tables and tall palms frame the bed, while a Louis XVI bench stands at its foot. Also in attendance is a claw-footed ivory chair from India.*

A HOUSE ON NEWPORT BAY

Almost everything about this weekend retreat is unconventional. The oceanfront lot, on a man-made island in Newport Bay, is narrow and oddly shaped. In addition to being a second home, the house is a second office, and to compound the unconventionality, Mr. and Mrs. Fred Carr, the owners, called an interior designer before they consulted an architect.

John Cottrell of Los Angeles was that interior designer, and he too is unusual in at least one sense. Unlike many other designers, he does not believe that his work should be exactly a "collaboration" with his clients. "It is my belief that an interior designer is a creator," he explains. "If owners have confidence in their designer, they should give him a free hand." In this case his point of view is not as arbitrary as it sounds; this is the second home he has designed for the Carrs, and it is obvious that he enjoys their complete confidence. Since they have remained close friends, the Carrs reversed the usual procedure and asked Mr. Cottrell to help find the right architect for their Balboa home.

The house had to meet certain specialized requirements as Mr. Carr wanted it to serve as his second office. Like many corporate executives, he had been in the habit of traveling extensively. Wishing to eliminate as much of this travel as possible, he decided to build a beach house with guest suites so that business associates could come to him.

While he discussed his particular requirements with Mr. Cottrell, the search for an architect was under way. For their purposes they needed an architect with a fresh approach, one unfettered by preconceived ideas about beach houses. Both the owners and the interior designer knew they had found the right man the moment they saw photographs of some houses William O'Dowd had designed and built in Portugal—houses which, in the architect's words, "spiral right out of the earth." These homes, created for a warm seaside climate, would be equally appropriate on a California bay. For the Carr house Mr. O'Dowd made extensive use of natural materials. Exposed and sandblasted beams are part of the dynamics of the design, as are courtyards, thick walls and expanses of sun-baked stucco.

For a beach house the result is quite original—unusually large, encompassing some ten thousand square feet of space. Walled on three sides, it is open in front to a panorama of boats sailing in the channel and yachts moored nearby. Within the house spatial relationships are dramatized and the ceiling height soars to thirty feet in the main living area. Generosity is the theme, and there are six fireplaces, four spiral staircases and four skylights. Each room has a patio, a balcony or a sun deck, while each guest suite has its private bedroom, sitting room, fireplace and bath. For a change of pace, there is a sunken conversation area, completely without an outside view. Even the swimming pool offers an innovative surprise, with a table and slab seats submerged at the shallow end. The art collection, too, is somewhat out of the ordinary, mixing the work of Dine and Calder and Miró with drawings by the Carrs' children.

John Cottrell has made every effort to make the interior décor conform to the generous thrust of architectural space and, at the same time, has taken into account all aspects of the owners' requirements. In particular he enjoyed using the children's art. "I like its honest spontaneity quite as much as I dislike a carefully calculated look. I prefer a beautifully composed collection of lovely things, which is just what we have here." To show his pleasure in the final result, he signed his name above the front door the day the house was completed.

RIGHT: *In a courtyard, sunlight and shadow impose ephemeral stripes on a Mexican fountain.* BELOW: *An intimate room—known familiarly as "the cave"—is a favorite after-dinner retreat. A triad of narrow vertical windows, a wine storage wall and a niche for firewood reinforce the architectural interest of the sunken Conversation Area, warmed by suede upholstery, fur pillows and rug.* OPPOSITE: *A view through the spiral staircase leading to the mezzanine reveals the decorative effect of exposed beams.*

OPPOSITE: *In the Mezzanine Living Area, the exposed beams form a complex weblike design overhead, adding a dark super-structure to the predominantly light space. Rosy-hued patterned sofa and wing chairs complement rustic accessories, including an ox yoke, a metal tub and straw baskets, above the long horizontal mantel. The result is an Early American atmosphere that contrasts boldly with the contemporary architecture.*

OPPOSITE BELOW: *Surrounded by small conversation groupings, a massive billiard table dominates the center of the ample space. An antique of puzzling origin, the table bears this mysterious inscription: "1873 custom-made for millionaire Posey." Around the room, large expanses of glass afford a choice of views: At right the bay is visible, while doors behind the billiard table open to a terrace overlooking the swimming pool and brick-paved barbecue area.*

ABOVE: *A tall built-in bookcase emphasizes the soaring height of the mezzanine living area, which can also function as a study. Reaching upward toward the structural beams, a large plant in a wooden tub repeats the vertical thrust of the bookcase. The spindle-back armchair, in the foreground, extends the Early American theme.*

OPPOSITE: *Vibrant upholstered chairs, with lively needle-point motifs designed by Diane Carr, add verve to the Dining Area. The bar at right can double as the children's soda fountain. The warm-toned brick flooring extends to the patio, linking indoor and outdoor environments.*

BELOW: *In the Kitchen and Breakfast Area, straw applied to wet plaster walls produces a rural effect reminiscent of French country cottages. A dark-beamed ceiling, hanging copper utensils, natural wood tones and straw baskets heighten the resemblance.*

FAR LEFT, ABOVE AND BELOW: *Antique appointments and a colorful fabric — used for draperies, bedcovering and chair upholstery — infuse the Master Bedroom with a harmonious warmth. The whimsical carpet, each square brightened by a provincial motif, is Portuguese. A child's cradle placed beside a chaise bergère is used in lieu of a table to hold magazines or flower arrangements.*

ABOVE LEFT: *Mirrors exaggerate the number of lamps illuminating a plant-filled Guest Bath, where a pair of Chinese covered jars stands out against light-colored tile.* LEFT: *Textural variety plays an important role in the décor of a guest suite Sitting Room, with crisp rattan and bamboo furniture and luxurious carpeting. A mirror behind the sofa discloses such details as a wood-beamed ceiling and a curved fireplace wall.* ABOVE RIGHT: *From a staircase below, a skylight creates an interesting organic pattern.* RIGHT: *A Sun Deck illustrates the aesthetic quality of William O'Dowd's architectural design.*

133

At night the house, surrounded by the bay and by tile-rimmed pools, resembles a multidecked floating ship. Its inner structure of wooden beams assumes a skeletal appearance—or shows itself in another sense: as the armature of a vast sculpture.

ECHOES OF THE 1930s

Michael Vincent lives at the northeastern edge of San Francisco, where Telegraph Hill rises steeply from the narrow fringe of piers and warehouses rimming the bay. Visitors must climb a shaded and winding stairway to the interior designer's home, which is hidden behind cascades of ivy.

The small entryway, white walled, brick paved and cool with the green of ferns, says little of the house beyond. One sees only an opaque glass door, and past that a twist of stairs. Then, abruptly, there is a long, sunlit space, a pale expanse of polished oak flooring and French doors opening to a view of San Francisco Bay. The vista encompasses a great breadth of blue water and sails, the far hills above Berkeley and the slow, eastward drift of clouds. No concern for the Victorian origin of the house could equal the force of this panorama. "The incredible view made me think of some deluxe suite on the *Normandie*," Michael Vincent recalls, and with that concept his design ideas came very easily. A narrow deck, later to be railed with white canvas, ran the length of the house and turned the northern corner. With minor structural alterations, Mr. Vincent laterally opened each of the three main rooms overlooking the bay. Then, by mirroring the southern interior wall, he doubled the illusion of length.

But no matter how splendid the panorama, there is an uncomfortable feeling in living on a cliffside ledge. It proved inadvisable to emphasize the long deck too greatly, and after several months' residence, the designer had the entire west wall of the living room mirrored. The visual doubling of the space supplied a necessary relief from the impact of the view, and a sense of openness in the opposite direction — created, ironically enough, by a duplication of the view itself. The mirrored living room wall was also made more important by the restoration of the fireplace, and by the placement of a large framed mirror over the mantel. The mirror, an oddity of redwood, which the designer describes as "Teddy Roosevelt country house," reflects a good deal of Mr. Vincent's personal taste. He likes objects that are a bit strange, often ones that have been overlooked. Of one small chair in the corner he says, "I remember very well that it was under a rainspout when I found it, with water pouring all over it."

Most of his similar discoveries are altered appreciably in function, finish or style of fabric. The chair, for example, has been cushioned with African mud cloth; the redwood mirror frame is bleached to a tone that closely matches the floor. The pleasing result of such transformations is a surprisingly sophisticated harmony of rough, even crude, materials with unabashedly glamorous design ideas.

Built firmly into the side of the hill, the bedroom is open only on the north side, where window walls lead to a stone-paved porch beneath the deck, and to a terrace beyond. Because this room is at all times cool, sections of the walls are a warm shade of terra-cotta. Large mirrors, one on the porch and several in the bedroom, bring into an otherwise dim chamber whispers of light and shadow and sunlit images of the flowers that cover the terrace wall. In the evening, as guests gather for cocktails in the rooms above, the sun shines gold in the windows across the bay, changing to rose in the haze against the hills. When the sky turns deep blue, Mr. Vincent lights the Chinese lantern in the dining room. From the Embarcadero it looks like a delicate pink moon hovering against the darkness of the hill.

The magnificent view is always at hand, but at no time is it overpowering. Michael Vincent never forgets that his house is a setting for people, rather than things. Laughter, happiness and comfort reign.

Designer Michael Vincent's compact home on Telegraph Hill, with its sweeping view of San Francisco Bay, reminds him of a deluxe suite aboard an elegant 1930s ocean liner. PRECEDING PAGE: Exotic elements — particularly Ami Magill's folding screen — also recall junglescapes by Henri Rousseau. Jute tapestry covers the Victorian steel folding chair; bleached redwood roots frame a mirror reflecting the night-time view; a twig stool lends another rustic touch.

ABOVE: One wall of mirror meeting another of bleached oak paneling trimmed with chrome molding adds stream-lined length to the Living Room. To the same end, a giant clamshell mounted on a massive pedestal exemplifies the use of overscale objects to augment the sense of space. Amid these vista-expanding devices, Portuguese spool-turned chairs surround a card table replicating a period design by Jean Michel Frank; orchids and a New Zealand flax plant serve to soften corners.

ABOVE: *Extending the 1930s mood, a plaster bas-relief from the 1939 Golden Gate International Exposition and a chrome-trimmed banquette occupy a shallow niche in the Living Room. Nearby, an Ashanti stool and a tree-bark planter flank a leather and tubular chrome armchair.* LEFT: *The living room's glazed ceramic console, ornamented with a sea horse motif, has an intriguing history: Originally it was an architectural detail that adorned the façade of a San Francisco fish market.*

The Dining Room commands a view of fingerlike piers and warehouses stretching into the bay, the far-reaching span of the Oakland Bay Bridge, and the spectacular backdrop of the Berkeley Hills and a cloud-streaked sky. Inside, a Chinese lantern seems to hover overhead.

In the Master Bedroom, a gilded Napoleon III mirror—
set off, like a theater stage, by draperies—reflects a witty
mise-en-scène climaxed by an Erté lithograph. The
pencil drawing next to the bed is by Michael Barnes,
and the gouache of an Indian is by Charles Frazier.

NORTHERN CALIFORNIA ELEGANCE

"A cottage," says Jack Lowrance. "That's what it was at the beginning." The description scarcely seems to apply to the elegant house in Woodside, near San Francisco, that the interior designer spent a year and a half completing. But if it is a cottage, it is a special one: filled with antiques, a rare collection of Oriental porcelain and other far-from-rustic accessories. More accurately, it is a cottage of the mind, a metaphor that is appropriate and pleasing to the owners who chose it for their retirement years.

In a profession that is occasionally ostentatious, Mr. Lowrance is given to understatement. "I never try to impose my own ideas," he hastens to say, seated behind a desk in the top-floor office of his Spanish-style house in Los Angeles, its panoramic view suggesting the hill towns of Italy. It is true enough that he may not have imposed his ideas on the owners of the Woodside house, but he certainly did guide them with notable firmness into several areas they had not anticipated. There were no conflicts, however, and the designer remembers the project as a continual pleasure. The owners, in his view, "have a flair for living." For this reason, and because they already owned most of the irreplaceable antiques now in the house, his task was a thoroughly pleasant and relatively easy one.

In the beginning he was brought in simply to supervise the selection of rugs and draperies, and no provision had been made for "decorating" as such. The owners thought it unnecessary, since they maintained, with a certain determination, that the house was no more than a "retirement cottage." The description was misleading, of course, and inaccurately summarized the active people who were to live in it and the formal way of life that they had been enjoying. Embracing some six thousand square feet, the house is small—at least in comparison with

others in which the owners had lived. They had spent long periods in the Orient, where they had become accustomed to generous space and omnipresent servants. Naturally, they thought of their retirement home in different terms. It became Mr. Lowrance's task to reconcile their contradictory wishes: a desire for simplicity and carefree living, and the maintenance of a sophisticated and elaborate way of life long familiar to them.

For example, their large collection of Ming and Japanese blue-and-white china demanded some appropriate setting. So the designer based a large part of the color scheme of the house on these rare treasures, and blue and white dominate much of the décor. These colors are especially effective in the gazebo and remodeled pool area, where the owners often entertain and dine alfresco. Little by little, Jack Lowrance, who does not "impose my own ideas," introduced a number of elements the owners had not considered. They had preferred a muted and monochromatic background; he gave them color. They did not want plants in the house; he managed to smuggle one into the dining room. And soon they wanted more. Aware and sophisticated people, they quickly realized what the designer was trying to do. He was reproducing for them, albeit on a somewhat more modest scale, the luxurious way of life that had been theirs for many years.

When is a cottage not a cottage? Clearly, it is not one when there are at least ten different and equally luxurious table settings and when the owners dine quietly at home in a room filled with rare appointments, and drink wine from eighteenth-century crystal. Mr. Lowrance found the need for this sort of elegance quite understandable, and he carefully created the décor of the Woodside house as an appropriate reflection of the owners themselves.

OPENING PAGE: *The contrasting themes of simplicity and grandeur are reconciled in Jack Lowrance's design for a Woodside cottage. A gilt-framed Degas drawing and the owners' collection of antique seals are displayed near a Ch'ien Lung lamp in the Living Room.*

OPPOSITE TOP: *Plant-screened windows and an Edo Period landscape screen bring the out-of-doors into the living room.* OPPOSITE CENTER: *The Dining Room table sparkles with miniature treasures, including small floral porcelains and winsome gilded figurines.* OPPOSITE BOTTOM LEFT: *In the Master Bedroom, Chinese and Japanese objets d'art are displayed in an 18th-century French cabinet.* OPPOSITE BOTTOM CENTER: *Small blanc-de-chine figures are ensconced in the niches of an 18th-century English lacquered secretary in the living room.* OPPOSITE BOTTOM RIGHT: *An Edo Period screen and a Louis XV sculpture of a theater page lend an eclectic air to the dining room.* ABOVE AND RIGHT: *The spacious master bedroom enjoys a verdant view and easy access to the swimming pool. Indoor comforts include a fireplace and a generous sitting area. A grouping of small lapis, jade, rock crystal and rhodolite fish rests on a table at the foot of a tassel-trimmed canopy bed.*

PRECEDING PAGES: *A blazing fire kindles a glow of warmth in the mahogany-paneled Library. Eighteenth-century bronze opium weights adorn the mantel, above which hangs a whimsical 19th-century painting-within-a-painting. The polished wood of a 19th-century English desk and the deep tones of a Bokhara rug enhance the cozy atmosphere.*

Mr. Lowrance designed two latticed structures for the garden behind the house. TOP ROW: *A Pergola extending from the living and dining rooms adds space to these areas. Profusely planted with flowers, it provides a gardenlike setting for before- and after-dinner entertaining.* BOTTOM LEFT: *A Patio for alfresco dining is painted with a trompe l'oeil scene of the mountains surrounding Woodside. A wittily placed mirror increases the visual complexity.* BOTTOM CENTER AND RIGHT, AND OPPOSITE: *The Gazebo, at one end of the swimming pool, houses an extensive collection of Imari porcelains. Inside, upholstery fabric repeats the Imari colors.*

CAPTURING ANOTHER ERA

Gleaming white, Italianate, the Henry Casebolt house on the hilltop was *the* manor of the neighborhood when it was completed in 1864. That neighborhood has changed considerably in the past century, and it is now the choicest of San Francisco residential locales. The Casebolt cow pastures, barn and windmill are gone, along with their rustic lake with waterfall and island. Yet with its hilltop situation and substantial scale, the house still dominates its surroundings, a picturesque presence among its more conventionally handsome neighbors.

It is the sort of house to weave Gothic tales about, and it seems appropriate that the present owner is a young romantic who never doubted, from the moment she came upon the then-occupied house, that it would someday be hers. She is Diane Burn, and she has created in the old Casebolt house an intimate sense of place, really an enchanting anachronism. Out of a nineteenth-century family home, built to accommodate eleven children, she has made a fantasy world that recalls earlier felicities.

Here is an eighteenth-century French country kitchen with time-stained, crumbling stucco walls and handpainted beamed ceiling; a dining room that suggests a Renaissance courtyard; a living room that is more a ballroom, all eighteenth-century boiseries and mirrored panels. And then there is her own bedroom, the stuff of storybooks, with two hundred yards of gauze flowing from a baldachin over the bed. It is a house in which one sheds disbelief at the door and steps into high romance.

It all began some years ago when Miss Burn, a native westerner who had made San Francisco her home, discovered "my house on the hill." It had been occupied by the same family for forty years, but nevertheless, every once in a while she would drive by for another glimpse. Almost inevitably, it

now seems, a For Sale sign appeared one day, and at last she was able to enter the house whose interiors she could already imagine.

Once inside, however, she discovered that the reality beyond the door had nothing to do with the exterior. "The interiors were the worst example of Victorian I'd ever seen in my life," she declares. But she was determined to have it: "I had dreamed of having this house. I just *knew* it was my house." Confident of her own intuition, she put her whole heart into the renovation for three years, in no hurry to complete anything—indeed, in no hurry to end the process of shaping the interiors of the house she loves. For Miss Burn the design process is always a highly charged emotional experience.

Her favorite aspects of interior design are the structural and interior finishes. It is the creation of the finished shells of the rooms that she finds most appealing, and her preferred materials are ephemeral wall washes, *faux-marbre* painted fantasies, eighteenth-century painted boiseries, walls of mirror, tented and handpainted ceilings. Her rooms are steeped in romance, and the romance is underscored by her choice of lighting. Wherever possible she uses candles, and all the period chandeliers are on dimmers to create the look of candlelight.

She does not feel burdened by the usual practical considerations of setting and furniture placement, or the routine niceties of the hostess who gives dinners for eight. Guests might be invited to stroll through the formal Italianate dining room and on to the eighteenth-century country kitchen, where they are comfortably seated on wood benches flanking the heavy table. With a fire glowing in the hearth and candles flickering overhead, it is easy to fall into the spirit of another age. Miss Burn's house is indeed a dance to the music of time.

PRECEDING PAGE: *Majestic vine-covered palms and a flourishing garden create a verdant frame for designer Diane Burn's 32-room Italianate dream home in San Francisco's Pacific Heights. Though completed in 1864, the height of the Victorian era, its stylistic influences were Neo-Classical and Renaissance Revival.*

ABOVE: *A view into the Living Room reveals the designer's use of architectural detailing to enhance the romantic effect.* BELOW AND RIGHT: *Eighteenth-century-style boiserie, painted in pastel shades, adds delicate drama to the high-ceilinged living room; period French furniture and an 18th-century boudoir screen extend the softly feminine look.*

ABOVE: *Imagination takes flight in the fanciful Solarium. Whimsical 19th-century-style garden murals, a latticework ceiling and a* **faux-marbre** *floor suggest a floral bower for morning repasts taken at an English bistro table. The 19th-century Parisian pastry counter appears perfectly at home in this confectionlike atmosphere.*

RIGHT: *A baronial grandeur permeates the Dining Room, where a bountifully laden table, resting on 18th-century inlaid marble bases, promises a feast fit for Lucullus. An ornate background continues the Italianate tone: Walls are washed with* faux - marbre *veining and the floor, designed by Ted Eden and painted by Ami McGill, simulates marble inlay.*

LEFT: *An 18th-century sandstone and carved-wood fireplace, from a château in Bourgogne, endows the Kitchen with a French provincial character. Harvest baskets heaped on a Parisian* Belle Epoque *baker's table and a swan painting by Ami McGill reinforce the rustic mood.*

ABOVE: *Sunlight streams through the kitchen's 19th-century Italian windows, illuminating artist Sean McVey's effective aged-stucco wall treatment. Another light source is a 19th-century French chandelier, originally in a winery, that now hangs appropriately above an 18th-century oak vintner's table. A floor of terra-cotta tile and a painted and wood-beamed ceiling contribute a mellow feeling, while an 18th-century Pierrot peers out from his cozy perch on the mantel.*

LEFT: *Artist Ami McGill's talent for delicate animal imagery is again expressed in the Master Bedroom. Here, she has adorned the hardwood floor with garland-entwined whippets reminiscent of Medieval tapestries.* BELOW LEFT: *The designer's playful sense of history is evident even in the Master Bath, where a French draped bath hanging screens a Directoire copper tub.*

OPPOSITE: *An aura of fairy-tale enchantment suffuses the master bedroom, where 200 yards of unbleached gauze drift from the baldachin of a Louis XV lit à la polonaise. Candles and firelight—the designer's favored forms of illumination—cast a golden glow, augmenting the romantic spirit.*

CREDITS

WRITERS

The following writers prepared the original *Architectural Digest* articles from which the material in this book has been adapted:

Lawrence Bouquet

Sam Burchell

George Christy

Alex Davis

Lois Wagner Green

Laurie Lewis

Ruth Miller

Suzanne Stark Morrow

Camilla Snyder

All original text adapted by Sam Burchell.

Caption Writers:

Joanne Jaffe

Joyce Madison

Joyce Winkel

PHOTOGRAPHERS

Jerry Bragsted 50-55

James Chen 96-101

Max Eckert 40-43, 44-49, 142-149

Leland Lee 88-95

Sheldon Lettich 74-79

Russell MacMasters 16-23, 32-39, 56-61, 62-73, 80-87 102-105, 136-141, 150-159

Timothy Street-Porter 10-15

Fritz Taggart 24-31, 122-135

Charles White 106-113, 114-121

DESIGN

Design Direction:

Philip Kaplan, Graphics Director

The Knapp Press

Book Design and Production:

Design Office/San Francisco

Bruce Kortebein

Cynthia Croker

Leigh McLellan